Stop Smoking

How To Conquer Your Smoking Addiction And Strategies To Quit For Good

(How To Quit Smoking And Live Without Nicotine Dependence)

Leandro Huffman

TABLE OF CONTENT

Introduction 1

How To Minimize Stress 19

Smoking's Effects On Health 28

Living A Life Without Tobacco – Benefits And Milestones 45

Adjusting To Withdrawal Symptoms 56

Managing Your Cravings 60

How To Stop: A Step-By-Step Guide 65

Make Wholesome Selections 67

How To Stop Smoking When Under Duress 79

The Benefits Of Smoking 85

Why Stop Smoking? How? And Right This Minute! 116

What Is The "Right" Way To Stop Smoking? 146

Introduction

There are at least one billion smokers worldwide. For smokers over the age of thirty, smoking may reduce their life expectancy by an average of five to six hours per day. And this is the robust life, not the old age life. Compared to non-smokers, smokers experience a greater number of debilitating illnesses in old age.

Even in this day and age, some people continue to wonder why they will cease smoking. Tobacco use causes both illness and mortality. It is likely the most modifiable lifestyle factor influencing human health. Every organ in the body is compromised by smoking. The heart, lungs, blood vessels, and fertility are all negatively impacted by tobacco use and cigarette compounds.

The nicotine added to cigarettes by cigarette manufacturers is highly addictive. When you begin to cease smoking, you will receive numerous advantages. You will be able to breathe more effectively than before. You will no longer be at risk for lung cancer, and you will also smell healthier. Additionally, you can save money because you will no longer purchase cigarettes.

If you wish to quit smoking, you will encounter difficulty. This is because you may experience anxiety, tension, an increased appetite, frustration, lethargy, or difficulty sleeping after discontinuing it. There are a variety of suggestions on the market for quitting smoking. Some are correct and others are incorrect. In this book, I have outlined some helpful strategies for quitting smoking. This will help you successfully eliminate this detrimental habit from your life.

I hope that you appreciate it!

Pharmaceutical commodities

Nicotine patches are a popular option for individuals attempting to quit smoking.

Tobacco contains more than 4,000 harmful compounds. Nicotine is one of the substances that contribute to tobacco addiction.

The purpose of nicotine replacement products is to help you gradually withdraw from nicotine. They provide a small quantity of nicotine to alleviate withdrawal symptoms. halting the replacement product is simpler than halting the individual strategy.

There are numerous varieties of nicotine replacement products, with the most common being:

Nicotine saliva

Nicotine nasal spray

Nicotine patch and inhalation device

Generally, the proper use of such products is the key to quitting for good. Let's examine an illustration of how it works:

Stage 1:

Before using nicotine replacement products, you must quit smoking.

Stage 2:

To manage your cigarette addictions, use nicotine replacement therapy (after consulting a professional about the most effective product and dosage for you).

Reduce the quantity in accordance with the program you are following.

Stage 3:

In the interim, seek out and initiate a support program, such as group therapy or counseling. Ensure that you disclose your use of nicotine replacement products during your counseling sessions so that the two treatments can complement one another. Set an objective of quitting cigarettes and nicotine replacement therapy within three to six months.

Consult a qualified expert to determine which product is most likely to aid you. Move and see your doctor; he or she will be able to advise you or refer you to a smoking cessation expert who is familiar with the correct use of nicotine replacement products.

Know the advantages

Determine the health benefits of ceasing smoking. If you effectively complete this research, you will be motivated to quit smoking. I have discovered, with your assistance, the unanticipated health benefits of quitting smoking. Let's examine:

After twenty minutes of inactivity:

The heart rate falls.

After twelve hours of abstinence

Blood carbon monoxide levels return to normal.

Two weeks to three months following cessation

Heart attack risk begins to decline, and lung function begins to improve.

One to nine months following cessation

Decreased wheezing and breathlessness.

A year after giving up

The risk of coronary heart disease is halved compared to a smoker.

Five years after leaving a job

Reduced risk for stroke.

After ten years of retirement

The lung cancer mortality rate is roughly half that of smokers. Mouth, esophagus, larynx, bladder, pancreas, and kidney cancers become less likely.

After fifteen years of retirement

The risk of coronary heart disease returns to the level of a nonsmoker.

Managing withdrawal signs

When your body is addicted to nicotine, you may go through some withdrawal symptoms when you stop smoking. I have already provided the names of the withdrawal symptoms in chapter one. Now let's see how you will overcome this:

Remind yourself that these feelings are temporary.

Reduce caffeine by avoiding or limiting soda, coffee, and tea.

Participate in a physical activity, such as going for a walk.

Try meditation or other relaxation techniques, such as soaking in a hot bath, receiving a massage, or taking long nose breaths.

Invite a friend and make plans for brunch, a concert, a movie, or other enjoyable activities.

Identify your specific emotions when you appear to be melancholy.

Feeling lonely, exhausted, boring, or hungry? Focus on these specific requirements.

Inhale thoroughly.

Enhance your level of physical activity. This will enhance your disposition and alleviate your depression.

If your weight gain is a concern, you may wish to consult a nutritionist or dietitian.

Medications

Bupropion

Under the brand name Zyban®, the antidepressant drug bupropion is used to treat nicotine addiction. The FDA gave its approval in 1997. This medication is suitable for use with nicotine replacement therapies. The bupropion reduces both nicotine withdrawal symptoms and nicotine addiction. Multiple adverse effects are associated with this product. Consult with your physician before using it.

Varenicline

Under the brand name Chantix®, the antidepressant drug varenicline is used to assist cigarette smokers in quitting the habit. It received FDA approval in 2006

By blocking nicotine's pleasurable effects and preventing nicotine cravings, this medication can assist those who wish to cease smoking. Consult your physician before using varenicline.

Start the day without smoking

The morning can establish the tone for the remainder of the day. Alter your morning routine and divert your attention away from smoking. Ensure that there are no cigarettes available. Before you go to bed, create a list of the things you must avoid the following morning that will make you want to smoke. Place this inventory where you previously stored cigarettes. Start each day with a well-planned activity that will keep you occupied for at least an hour. It will help keep your mind and body occupied, preventing you from thinking about smoking. Each day should begin with deep respiration and at least one glass of water.

Go to support center

There are numerous detox and support centers in our society. You are able to visit a single center for guidance. It will assist you in quitting smoking.

How To Minimize Stress

While attempting to quit smoking, it is advisable to eliminate as many stressful situations as feasible. You must first determine the actual causes of your stressful circumstances. It is difficult because the sources of your stress are not always readily apparent and can be easy to neglect. Sometimes, as adults, we add to our own tension in the workplace, particularly through procrastination. People frequently neglect this and mistakenly attribute stress to their workplace when, in reality, this is rarely the case. If you maintain a stress journal and record every time you feel stressed, you will be better able to pinpoint the sources of your stress.

People smoke when they are agitated, and stress may be the leading cause of smoking. Smoking dulls the experience of living. Therefore, in order to resign more effectively, improved stress management skills are required. Taking a few minutes to relax is one strategy for coping with a stressful situation. Exit the building and take several long breaths. If possible, perform games or speak with a friend. You could also indulge in a snack or indulgence. These activities can improve your ability to deal with stressful situations.

Exercise. This cannot be overemphasized. If everyone exercised as they should, I believe that half of the world's health problems would disappear (well, not really, but I like to imagine they would). In addition to pumping blood throughout the body, exercise releases mood-enhancing chemicals in the brain, such as dopamine and oxytocin, which reduce tension. If you do not run, you could simply meander. A daily walk of 30 minutes in the fresh air will greatly reduce your tension levels.

Meditation is another option. Do not believe that only Buddhists in the Far East practice meditation. Meditation is advantageous for everyone because it modifies the neural pathways in the brain and enables you to think more clearly and be happier. Simply sit up straight on the floor, close your eyes, and clear your consciousness of all distractions. Concentrate on a single task to eliminate all tension. Just make sure that your primary focus is not smoking.

Lastly, chuckle. Laughter is the greatest medicine, as it has been shown to reduce the stress hormone cortisol while increasing mood-boosting chemicals such as endorphins. Therefore, be with your companions and laugh. Find a funny internet jest and chuckle. Bring up your beloved comedies on Netflix and YouTube and have a good time!

Stopping abruptly

Although this method appears to be the most appealing route to nicotine liberation, it is not suitable for everyone. Moreover, not everyone succeeds. According to research, only a small percentage of individuals who quit smoking cold turkey are successful on their first try. Some argue that it is less efficacious than placebo medications. Think about it before labeling these studies as false and researching the charlatan who funded them. What are the effects of discontinuing a drug? Withdrawal indicators. When you abruptly stop smoking, particularly if you've been a smoker for years, you may experience withdrawal symptoms that hinder your ability to perform daily tasks. This is why it is the most prevalent method for quitting smoking, but also the least effective. Are we advising you against quitting cold turkey? Of course not. If you believe you can, you should certainly attempt it.

The initial step in quitting cold turkey is realizing what you are entering into. There will be symptoms associated with this method that will hinder your ability to perform certain duties. These symptoms may include fatigue, irritability, tremors, and fatigue. In the first few days, they will be extremely potent, but will gradually diminish thereafter. Therefore, if you are able to endure the initial onslaught of symptoms, this method may be for you.

The second stage in quitting is to develop an exit strategy. People mistakenly believe that quitting cold turkey means discontinuing without any preparation. You should plan as much as possible in life, and ceasing smoking cold turkey is no exception. Choose a date on which you intend to cease smoking, and then record on a calendar each day you have been smoke-free. Ensure that the day you choose to cease falls during a period in which you are less likely to cave to your cigarette cravings. You must identify everything in your life that compels you to smoke. Is it anxiety? Are they your friends? Does it attend parties? After identifying them, you should take precautions to avoid them. Obviously, you do not want to cease hanging out with your friends, but you should avoid situations where they will be smoking. If that is unavoidable, you could request that they refrain from smoking in your presence. Those who are your friends will comprehend. Throughout this entire procedure, you must continually remind yourself of why you halted in order to avoid having to restart. Reminding yourself will maintain your motivation. You could carry a journal or diary with you and record every day how your body feels.

The final step in successfully quitting using the cold turkey method is to manage your tension levels effectively. Nicotine has a tranquil effect and allows you to forget about your problems. This is why, following a stressful day, people smoke cigarettes to relax. If you want to cease, you will need to develop new stress management strategies. Take lengthy walks, read a book, listen to soothing music, or engage in physical activity. These are general methods by which an individual can eliminate tension naturally.

Again, this method is not appropriate for everyone. If you find yourself relapsing, this is a sign that you need to discover an alternative method of quitting. Do not punish yourself for it. You attempted to quit, which is the most crucial step in the process.

Smoking's Effects On Health

Addiction, or, more accurately, dependence, is a significant negative health effect common to all forms of tobacco use. Fixation is not fatal in and of itself, but it contributes to tobacco-caused death and disease because it encourages smokers to continue their habit, which repeatedly exposes them to the toxins in tobacco smoke. Despite the fact that there are numerous verifiable records of the clear capacity of tobacco use to become a habit for certain smokers, it wasn't until after the 1980s that leading health organizations, including the Workplace of the Top health spokesperson in the US, the Imperial Society of Canada, and WHO, officially acknowledged that cigarettes are extremely habit-forming due to their capacity to deliver large amounts of nicotine into the lungs, from which blood is then drawn.

Nicotine produces the full spectrum of physical and behavioral effects associated with habit. These effects include the initiation of reward systems in the mind that have behavioral effects and physiological cravings that lead to persistent use, resistance and actual dependence, and withdrawal upon cessation. Additionally, nicotine's properties are enhanced by various components of tobacco smoke that, for some individuals, have delightful tangible properties. Smelling salts, menthol, levulinic corrosive, and, surprisingly, chocolate contribute to the flavor and aroma of cigarettes. Cigarettes are more irresistible than nicotine medications, such as nicotine patches and lozenge, whose tactile and distinct effects are more vulnerable and less appealing.

Deep inhalation of smoke containing nicotine results in rapid nicotine retention in the lungs; nicotine diffuses into the circulatory system as rapidly as oxygen. From the airways, nicotine reaches the brain in less than ten seconds. Neurons in the brain and peripheral sensory system have receptor proteins on their surfaces to which nicotine binds, similar to how a key fits into a lock. When a particle of nicotine binds to a nicotine receptor, it causes the neuron to transmit nerve impulses to various objective organs and tissues. This interaction stimulates the advent of synapses, or chemical messengers, which produce the physiological and mental effects of nicotine. For example, nicotine stimulates the adrenal glands and induces the release of epinephrine and norepinephrine, which are responsible for elevating pulse and circulatory tension as well as enhancing alertness and focus. Nicotine also stimulates the release of dopamine from synapses in the brain. Dopamine is believed to be essential to nicotine's uplifting and euphoric mood-altering effects.

The majority of smokers report that their initial experiences with nicotine were anything but pleasurable. The nicotine in tobacco can have detrimental effects on first-time users, who typically experience drowsiness, nausea, and vomiting. With practice, smokers become adept at regulating their nicotine intake to achieve the optimal effects. With continued tobacco use, however, the body produces an increasing number of nicotine receptors.

Thus, the smoker experiences a phenomenon known as nicotine tolerance, in which greater quantities of nicotine are required to achieve the same effect. When nicotine tolerance has developed and consumption has increased, the body becomes physiologically dependent on nicotine, and any abrupt cessation of smoking will result in withdrawal symptoms. These adverse effects include impaired cognitive function, irritability, weight gain, a depressed state of mind, tension, difficulty sleeping, and persistent cravings. The adverse effects typically peak within a few days and quickly subside. In any case, the experience varies from person to person, and, as far as some are concerned, intense desires can persist for a very long time.

Nicotine's ability to aid tobacco users in regulating their mood and appetite, as well as enhancing their concentration while working, undoubtedly contributes to the persistence of tobacco use. A portion of these effects relate to actual dependence. For instance, increased exposure to nicotine can increase actual dependence and thereby intensify the withdrawal symptoms. During withdrawal, resuming smoking alleviates withdrawal symptoms rapidly. This response may lead the smoker to believe that smoking itself enhances mood and performance, whereas the effect is primarily that of reversing the withdrawal symptoms that result from nicotine dependence. This effect can be substantial, depending on the smoker's perspective. For instance, cigarette smokers typically weigh 2 to 4 kg (4.4 to 8.8 pounds) less than nonsmokers, and weight gain is occasionally associated with quitting smoking. The resumption of smoking can help individuals lose weight. In essence, even a few lengthy periods of tobacco abstinence can render certain individuals incapable of completing their work, studying for an exam, or performing adequately in other areas. Eventually, a smoker may discover that a single cigarette is sufficient to restore immediate performance.

All commonly used tobacco products contain addictive levels of nicotine. However, the examples of causes that can lead to dependence vary among tobacco products and are influenced by numerous factors. For instance, increasing the price and restricting access to tobacco products will generally reduce tobacco use (thus reducing the risk of dependency) and may encourage some dependent individuals to quit smoking. Stogie smoking and pipe smoking are typically adopted later in life than cigarette smoking, and stogie smokers and pipe smokers are less likely to inhale the smoke. Consequently, the general rate of dependence on stogies or lines appears to be less than the rate for cigarettes, despite the fact that many stogie or line consumers become extremely dependent.

The greatest risk of nicotine dependence arises when the drug is retained rapidly, delivering its prominently pleasant psychoactive effects. Oral smokeless products, such as snuff and biting tobacco, have a slower effect on the mind than inhaling tobacco smoke, but the convenience and comfort of these products are appealing to many and contribute to their compelling effects.

Cancer

It is estimated that approximately 33 percent of all cancer deaths are attributable to tobacco use. More than sixty known carcinogens are present in tobacco smoke, including tobacco-specific nitrosamines and polycyclic fragrant hydrocarbons. Although certain body compounds utilize cancer-causing agents and cause them to be released, these catalysts occasionally function inadequately, allowing cancer-causing agents to bind to cell DNA and damage it. Tumors develop when cells with damaged DNA survive, proliferate, and aggregate. Dangerous cells can metastasize, or spread to other parts of the body, allowing the malignant growth to proliferate. As a result of the toxicity of tobacco products, malignancy risk is still uncertain; however, the risk of disease is also strongly related to the quantity and duration of toxin exposure.

The longer and more frequently an individual smokes, the greater the likelihood of developing a tobacco-related disease. Therefore, habit is a primary area of strength for a supporter of various diseases, as it promotes a high level and tenacious exposure to disease-causing agents.

Since the majority of tobacco consumers are cigarette smokers who inhale smoke into their lungs, it is not surprising that active smoking and exposure to natural tobacco smoke account for 90% of all cases of cellular disintegration in the lungs. In all nations of the world where smoking has increased, there has been an undeniable increase in cellular destruction in the lungs. In the United States, cellular breakdown in the lungs is responsible for more malignant growth deaths than any other disease and murders more women annually than breast cancer. It is estimated that 85% of all instances of cellular breakdown in the airways could be prevented if all cigarette smoking were to cease.

However, exposure to cancer-causing agents is not limited to the respiratory system. Tobacco use is a significant cause of bladder cancer, pancreatic disease, laryngeal disease, oral cancer, and esophageal cancer. When a typical tobacco user quits smoking, their risk of developing cancer decreases, but not to the extent of someone who has never smoked. Currently, smokeless tobacco users frequently expose the oral mucosa to toxins and have a significantly increased risk of developing head and neck malignancies; however, the danger is influenced by the length of use and the nature of the product. For example, Swedish smokeless tobacco ("snus") is manufactured to contain considerably lower levels of cancer-causing agents than American smokeless tobacco, and the risk of tobacco-caused cancer in its users appears to be proportionally lower. There are significant geographical differences in the prevalence of oral tobacco use, with higher prevalence in Sweden, India, Southeast Asia, and parts of the United States.

Lung Disease

It is not the norm for smokers to experience multiple respiratory infections in addition to cellular destruction of the lungs. One such condition is chronic obstructive pneumonic disease (COPD), which is one of the major causes of weakness and potential death in cigarette smokers. Over 80% of those diagnosed with COPD are smokers, and the overwhelming majority of these individuals die prematurely, with a greater proportion of women dying from COPD than men. COPD is an umbrella term for respiratory diseases in which airflow is obstructed. According to all accounts, the effects of tobacco smoke on women's aviation routes are more delicate. Women with COPD commonly experience greater breathlessness and a disproportionately greater thickening of airway passage walls than males with COPD. In most cases, COPD refers to persistent bronchitis (persistent hacking and mucous production) and emphysema (extremely persistent enlargement of air spaces joined by disintegration of lung walls), although specific symptomatic criteria can vary. Active smoking and exposure to environmental tobacco smoke are also responsible for increases in other respiratory diseases, such as pneumonia, the common cold, and influenza. It takes longer for smokers to recover from these illnesses than it does for nonsmokers. Children are particularly defenseless against the effects of environmental tobacco smoke. When children are raised in a family where they are constantly exposed to natural tobacco smoke, they are likely to develop asthma and chronic cough, and they may experience diminished lung development and function.

Cardiac Disease

For a long time, cardiovascular disease has been viewed as a significant risk associated with smoking, with the risk becoming greater the more one consumes. According to recent research, the carbon monoxide present in tobacco smoke binds to hemoglobin, reducing the number of blood cells that can transport oxygen. In addition, coronary blood flow is reduced, causing the heart to work harder to deliver oxygen to the body. This stress positions smokers at a substantially greater risk for myocardial fibrosis, coronary failure, and stroke. There are, however, regional and gender differences in the incidence of cardiovascular disease caused by smoking. In China, where approximately 53% of adult males smoke (compared to approximately 2.4% of adult females), cardiovascular disease accounts for a much smaller proportion of smoking-related deaths than in the United States and Europe, where it accounts for approximately 30 to 40% of all tobacco-caused deaths. Furthermore, research has demonstrated that even mild or moderate smoking (1 to 14 cigarettes per day) significantly increases the risk of sudden cardiovascular death in women. In the year following cessation, a smoker's risk for cardiovascular disease decreases faster than the risk for cellular disintegration in the lungs, and the risk reductions are evident.

IMPACTS ON PREGNANCY

Women who smoke will inevitably experience infertility and an unnatural delivery cycle (unrestrained fetus removal). When a pregnant woman smokes, certain toxins from the smoke can be transmitted to the infant. These toxins can later affect a child's lung development and capacity. Babies born to women who smoke are more likely to be conceived hastily, to have a low birth weight, and to have slower initial development. Smoking cessation during the first trimester reduces these health risks to levels comparable to those of

individuals who have never smoked.
Infants from families where t

Living A Life Without Tobacco – Benefits And Milestones

Negative effects of smoking are not something consumers are unaware of. However, are you aware of how hazardous it is? This book is intended to provide motivation to cease smoking, not frightening statistics that you may already be aware of. The most rewarding aspect of ceasing smoking is the permanent transformation of your life.

One Month of Quitting Successfully

- Your stamina will substantially increase, and you will be able to perform light to moderate exercise without experiencing shortness of breath.

- Your garments and natural body odor will be significantly better than when you smoked.

- Your smoking-dulled senses, such as taste and scent, will return to normal.

- Your teeth and cuticles will maintain their original hue.

Other Significant Milestones

- The beneficial effects of quitting smoking become apparent within the first twenty minutes, when your blood pressure and pulse rate return to normal after being elevated by smoking.

- Carbon monoxide levels in your body attain normal after 12 hours.

- Within three months and two weeks of quitting smoking, your respiratory functions and circulation return to normal.

- Within a year of ceasing successfully, your stamina recovers and you experience less shortness of breath. Your lungs become more open to deep, pure respiration.

- The risk of developing lung cancer can be cut in half within the first decade after ceasing smoking. Additionally, the risk of other malignancies decreases significantly.

Benefits of a Healthy Lifestyle

If the possibility of organic damage restoration does not motivate you, nothing will! Your body has sustained severe injury over the years. It is now time to undo the damage done and join the club for healthful living. Life is extremely valuable and should not be sacrificed for something as trivial as nicotine addiction. In addition to health benefits, ceasing smoking has several additional advantages.

- Profit monetarily by leaving

Did you realize how much damage smoking inflicts on your wallet? A straightforward calculation, which you have conveniently ignored for all these years, will reveal the amount of money you spend annually on cigarettes. You can save this money and use it as a reward each time you reach a significant milestone. Simply save the money in a jar, and when you have enough, indulge yourself to something more substantial.

- Adopt New Routines to Complement a Smoke-Free Lifestyle

It is a wonderful feeling to develop new habits after quitting smoking successfully. It depends on which gives you the greatest satisfaction: the weight you lost due to a healthy lifestyle or the marathon you ran with your community. As one's behaviors evolve, so does one's perception. You will regard your body with considerably more respect and prioritize long-term health objectives.

- Maintain authority over your social life

Have the option to join a social group that does not partake in smoking or similar diversions. Remember the times when your companions reacted negatively to the odor of smoke you brought with you or when you smoked in their presence? Breaking this addiction will grant you considerably more control over your social interactions.

- Serve as a model for someone

It requires a great deal of commitment to combat addictions and replace them with new behaviors. Perhaps your efforts and diligence in choosing health will convince someone else to do the same. You can serve as a positive example for those who choose to remain on the path to redemption. The best method to motivate someone to follow in your footsteps is to set a good example.

- Publicise your achievement

What you did is not everyone's strong suit. Against all odds, you chose to take that path, maintained your resolve, and accomplished what you set out to do! This is an outstanding accomplishment that merits praise. Utilize social media to make your effort and ensuing success known to your friends and family. This will assist you in maintaining your current lifestyle.

PART IV General Guidelines

Find out what works for you for any additional general advice I could offer. Hypnosis assisted me. It is not effective for everyone. Determine what works for you. If you quit smoking and then resume, don't consider it a failure; consider it feedback. Determine what did not work and attempt something else; if that does not succeed, try something else. And if that doesn't work, attempt another approach! Just keep trying. Most individuals require three, four, or five tries to complete a task. You can succeed! The most important thing is to decide to do it. Because I've done it, anyone can do it, including you.

Obtaining assistance is another tip. Tell people and make a public declaration that you will quit smoking on this date and that you need assistance, support, and people around you. You simply need someone who will get you through, say the appropriate words, and have some patience with you for a while. You will succeed if you surround yourself with a team that will provide support.

PART V Final Suggestion

My final piece of advice is to never say that you are quitting smoking, as you are not truly quitting anything. You are doing something amazing for yourself. To say "I'm giving up something" implies that you are prohibited from possessing it. It's as if you're depriving yourself, and what that does is implant a negative message in your subconscious mind. That message that you are unable to receive. And your subconscious mind will desire that object. Therefore, never state that you are giving up anything.

You are ceasing or stopping smoking, but you are not giving up.

CHAPTER SIX Closing

I trust that some of these tips were helpful. I wish you good fortune. My decision to stop smoking was the greatest thing I've ever done. I no longer desire a cigarette. I cannot picture myself smoking. I have never smoked and never will!

Chapter 4 - Identifying Your Triggers

Keeping track of your smoking triggers is essential for your success in ceasing. It is crucial that you identify the things or situations that trigger your desire to smoke. Keeping a journal of your cravings can assist you with this step. A week prior to your quit date, observe your smoking habits and maintain a log of them. Include details about the following:

The duration you inhaled

The severity of your hunger. A rating scale can be used to quantify intensity.

What were you doing while you were smoking?

Were you with a companion?

What emotions did you experience while smoking?

Did you experience any sensations after smoking?

To manage negative emotions such as depression, stress, dread, and anxiety, adults smoke. Although cigarettes can provide transient relief from these negative emotions, there are far healthier alternatives, such as meditation, exercise, or even simple breathing exercises.

Even if you successfully cease smoking, the emotions you used cigarettes to suppress will eventually return. Therefore, it is crucial that you learn to deal with these early on in the ceasing process.

Here are some reminders to help you avoid the most common smoking triggers:

At the conclusion of each meal. If you are one of those smokers who conclude each meal with a cigarette, the idea of abandoning this long-standing custom may initially seem daunting. Replace the cigarette with a healthy alternative, such as a healthy dessert, a piece of fruit, a stick of gum, or a small square of chocolate, to help you endure.

Alcohol. Many smokers consume intoxicating beverages while smoking. To eliminate this trigger, abstain from drinking alcohol as much as possible, or only consume in places where smoking is prohibited. You can also snack on chips and nuts, or gnaw on something like a cocktail stick or straw.

Others who smoke. If you have smoking acquaintances or family members, it is extremely difficult to resist the urge to smoke and avoid relapse signs. Inform them of your decision to stop smoking and request that they make some adjustments, such as refraining from smoking when you are around. On your own initiative, avoid forming relationships with only smokers. locate activities that can serve as a distraction, or locate someone who does not smoke with whom you can hang out.

Adjusting To Withdrawal Symptoms

As your body begins to withdraw from nicotine, physical withdrawal symptoms will begin to manifest once you have officially quit smoking. The withdrawal symptoms will peak two to three days after the last cigarette is smoked. Withdrawal symptoms typically commence within thirty minutes to one hour after the last cigarette is smoked and peak two to three days later. The symptoms vary from individual to individual and can last from a few days to weeks.

Despite the fact that these symptoms may be unpleasant, they are only temporary. As the toxins begin to be expelled from your system, the symptoms will gradually improve. But while you are experiencing one, explain to your family and friends that you may experience mood fluctuations from time to time, and ask for their patience as you go through this.

The most common nicotine withdrawal symptoms, their duration, and what you can do to alleviate them are detailed below.

An intense yearning for cigarette. This is the most severe symptom, peaking within the first week but persisting for a couple of months. You can attempt to distract yourself, or you can simply wait out the urge.

Impatience and acrimony. This could last between two and four weeks. To combat this, use relaxation techniques and avoid caffeinated products such as chocolate and coffee.

Insomnia is the inability to slumber. This could last between two and four weeks. Avoid consuming caffeine after six in the evening if you have this. Plan activities like perusing a book if you have trouble falling asleep.

Fatigue. Additionally, this can last between two and four weeks. Do not force yourself when you are exhausted, and take frequent, brief naps.

Inability to focus for an extended period of time. This may last several weeks. If you find it difficult to concentrate, reduce your responsibilities and avoid stress as much as possible.

Hunger. This can last for several weeks or longer. Choose to consume water or low-calorie liquids. Also, consume low-calorie munchies.

Nasal drainage, throat dryness, and wheezing. This could last for a few weeks. Cough drops can be used to alleviate wheezing. Additionally, it is advised that you consume plenty of water and other fluids.

Constipation and flatulence are two common digestive issues. This symptom may manifest within the first two weeks after quitting smoking. Increase your fiber consumption and fluid intake. Exercise also helps.

Managing Your Cravings

By avoiding triggers, you will be able to reduce your impulses. However, it cannot eliminate your appetites entirely. Remember that, as with all things, your cravings are temporary and will ultimately pass. While you can attempt to wait them out, you can also prepare for their arrival beforehand. Having a plan for dealing with your desires prevents you from giving in significantly.

You can first attempt to distract yourself. You can volunteer to do duties such as dishwashing and laundry. You can simply take a shower, turn on the television, or contact a friend to hang out if you're not interested. It does not matter what activity you choose, as long as it serves the purpose of diverting your thoughts away from smoke.

Additionally, it is always helpful to recall why you resigned in the first place. Consider the money you will save, the improvement in your health and appearance, and the boost to your self-esteem that will result from ceasing smoking.

In addition, if you find yourself in an environment that tempts you to revert to your old habits, make every effort to avoid doing so. Your current location and activities may be the cause of your desires, so a change of scenery can be of great assistance.

It is also effective to reward yourself for the daily victories you achieve. Remind yourself of these victories. Do not neglect to give yourself a nice reward to keep yourself motivated.

Additionally, you can attempt the following:

Consider something to ruminate on. When experiencing appetites, it is essential to have something in your mouth. These may include hard candy, mints, vegetables such as celery or carrot spears, sunflower seeds, and gum.

Keep your hands occupied as much as feasible. Give your hands a task to perform. Squeeze pencils, pellets, or paper clips to satisfy your need for tactile stimulation.

Please brush your teeth. This will give you a sense of cleanliness and freshness, which will likely eliminate your desire to smoke.

Be lively! Do some exercises. Walk through the park, perform yoga stretches, or jog. Stay physically active.

You can also attempt to unwind. Perform a relaxing activity, such as meditating, taking a heated bath, or reading a good book.

Conclusion

It is never too late to stop smoking, regardless of your age. Successfully quitting this addiction will not only benefit you and your body, but also those around you. By giving up smoking, you protect those you care about from the dangers posed by the compounds contained in each cigarette. When you decide to cease smoking, you may consult a physician, who will provide you with additional advice and suggestions, as well as the appropriate medication if necessary.

Again, thank you for downloading this book!

I hope that this book was able to help you discover a way to quit smoking permanently.

Please take the time to share your thoughts and post a review on Amazon if you enjoyed this book. It would be much appreciated!

Thank you and best wishes!

How To Stop: A Step-By-Step Guide

Those who have engaged in this vice for an extended period of time may find it difficult to cease cold turkey. In such a situation, the best course of action is to proceed cautiously and methodically.

SHRINKING IT DOWN

Consider smoking less cigarettes. If you smoke one pack per day, resolve to reduce your consumption by half. You must maintain this for at least one month. The following month, attempt to reduce it in half again, and so on. When you are down to one cigarette per day, you can begin the rapid method. Set a date and resign immediately.

SEEK MEDICAL SUPPORT

The alternative plan is to cease with the assistance of a physician. Request nicotine replacement therapy or a prescription medication to help you cease. Typically, physicians will first determine if you are capable of quitting cold turkey or if you require assistance. The majority of the time, they will recommend a progressive withdrawal process so that your body can adapt to the changes.

They may even prescribe you helpful supplements. Therefore, you can visit your physician, inform him of your intention to cease, and ask for guidance on how to do so.

.

Make Wholesome Selections

Typically, smoking is accompanied by another undesirable behavior. It could be imbibing or another activity. If you decide to cease smoking, you may as well make other healthy choices.

For instance, if you are a smoker and an alcoholic, you should attempt to cease both. This will provide greater gratification in the long run, as you will be able to overcome two obstacles simultaneously, and you will break the connection between drinking, smoking, and pleasure.

If you smoke while drinking coffee, consider switching to decaf while you quit. Drink a different flavor of tea, one that you have never combined with tobacco, so that you are not constantly reminded of smoking when you drink tea.

Exercise is a further addition to your healthful options. Enroll in a gym, dance class, martial arts club, or any other organization devoted to physical fitness. This provides you with a wholesome diversion, and physical activity makes you happy. Endorphins are feel-good hormones that are produced during exercise. Typically, tension and problems lead to the development of a smoking habit. Therefore, if you have an abundance of happy hormones, the desire to smoke (which can be provoked by negative emotions) will be suppressed.

A further healthful option is to avoid smoking individuals. Before deciding to avoid them, you should explain the reason why. They may be your acquaintances or family. It may surprise you to learn that they may want to resign but are waiting for someone else to initiate the process.

If you smoke due to stress, you should ascertain the source of your stress. Determine if it is something you can permanently alter or eliminate from your life once you have this information. Without the stimulus, it is also possible to control the craving.

If you smoke because of your job (for example, writers often smoke to help them concentrate), you can either replace smoking with something else, such as chewing gum, or, if possible, change your career.

Smoking destroys!

...

Chapter 5 Effects of Withdrawal

Withdrawal is likely the greatest obstacle that anyone battling addiction must surmount. The symptoms affect every aspect of your life, including your demeanor, behavior, and body in a manner that can be devastating.

As a result of the withdrawal effect, a significant number of former smokers have resumed their habit. Typically, the symptoms result from the absence of nicotine in the system. Even those using the step-by-step method and substituting cigarettes with patches, gum, lozenges, and mouth sprays will experience withdrawal symptoms, although they will be less severe than those experienced by someone discontinuing cold turkey.

So, what withdrawal symptoms can you anticipate when you stop smoking? You will become irritable and easily agitated in terms of behavior. You will also experience depressive and anxious episodes. You will have difficulties concentrating mentally. Some individuals have demonstrated restlessness that disrupts their slumber.

Physically, your heart rate will decrease, as will your adrenaline and cortisol levels. Simultaneously, your appetite may increase, causing weight gain.

These symptoms manifest 24 hours after quitting. After one week, you will experience the zenith of the effects. Typically, symptoms disappear within a month. Obviously, it may take up to six months for some individuals to begin to feel better.

In addition to wheezing, sore throat, earache, deafness, and feeling off-color, you may experience cold symptoms such as sneezing, headache, and mouth ulcers after quitting smoking. Additionally, you may encounter constipation, fatigue, and lethargy.

When you are compelled to inhale, Consider tasting a filthy ashtray. This is what I did, and it was successful.

I haven't smoked in years, but when I'm around other smokers, I still question, "Did I really smell like that?"

Now, the odor of smoke makes me nauseated.

THE IMPORTANTEST WORD

Do you know what the most essential word in existence is? No... not a rat. Ron Hubbard, a prominent American philosopher and practitioner and the founder of Scientology, asserts that this term is SURVIVE! I believe that putting this word at the top of your life will lead you to the philosophy of a lawyer lady who believes that cannibalism is justifiable under certain survival conditions.

I recollect a scene from a movie in which two ministers meet and one asks the other, "Do you know what is most crucial and challenging about our work?" It is the ability to restrict one's desires.

Do you recognize the word I'm referring to? No? This is the word NO.

Only when a person says NO to himself, limiting himself in these or other desires, and daily practicing a hateful "program"... will he be able to overcome his hatred. Only then is he able to say NO to external circumstances and continue on his path, without deviating or eating cheap gingerbread placed in a mousetrap.

Regarding marzipan. Do not eat after six, as the famous ballerina Maya Plisetskaya loved to say.

Well, let's get to the primary point.

HOW TO STOP SMOKING!

Record the recipe, as it is essential! The tested procedure has a duration of exactly one week.

Take a red brick, preferably one that is a week old, and smash it with a hammer into small fragments. Put it through the grinder... Oh no. This recipe is from my upcoming book. Therefore, we defer it until later.

HOW TO STOP SMOKING!

I elucidate without any preliminaries. Consider that you smoke one pack of cigarettes per day. Then you should double your "diet" intake. Thus, you must smoke 14 cartons per week.

And you purchase the incorrect brand of tobacco products, not the one you adore to your dying day, as well as various brands of cigarettes, the stronger the better. And further, eliminate your organism.

All of this must be accomplished with a smile. You are currently en route to treatment. And regardless of your circumstances, you must "get with the program." Yes, a thorough inhale is necessary to reach the filter.

Headache? Vomit? Your blood pressure has increased and your appetite has vanished? What are you saying? Nobody will feel sorry for you or stroke behind your ear. No one besides yourself needs you. From the topmost bell tower, this world doesn't care about you. And there will be no magical faerie, nor will she save you from disease. In addition, she has little regard for you and your phlegm. You will begin to contemplate non-smoked cigarettes on the seventh day of the program, with horror. You will feel terrible, worse than ever. Obviously, you will want to complete the program early. I do not recommend this, however. You do not want the universe to give you a thrill, do you? You must smoke the entire prescribed amount of tobacco to completion, regardless of the circumstances.

Excuses are unacceptable. The nuclear flash does not count if it occurs abruptly. You must adhere to the program regardless of external stimuli or an abrupt stomachache. On the eighth day, early in the morning, you will awaken... Oh, what a marvel! You have no desire for smoke. As a gesture of nostalgia, you may insert a cigarette butt into your ear. Joke:) Do you comprehend what I'm referring to? You are the cause, a clot of energy and power. You determine how your life will unfold. Even if everyone wipes their feet around you, the cloth will not leak orange juice.

The universe adores and aids those who are courageous. Dweebs have never been adored or respected by anyone. Because dweebs are dangerous, everyone always wishes to give them a magical kick to keep them away. Very hazardous. They'll sell out and betray you. They cannot be trusted or you cannot place any trust in them. Which side will you take, You, my friend? You determine. Regards from the new volume.

How To Stop Smoking When Under Duress

Still, the prospect of quitting for good may seem daunting, especially given that nicotine withdrawal symptoms include irritability and anxiety. In this case, you will need to find alternative, healthy ways to manage tension. Here are several methods for achieving this objective.

1. Solicit Assistance From a Support System

Director of clinical services at the University of Wisconsin Center for Tobacco Research and Intervention in Madison, Douglas Jorenby, Ph.D., says that seeking assistance from others — in the form of counseling, a formal smoking cessation program, or a text or telephone "quitline" — can often help a person deal with stress and anxiety. You may also discuss with your physician whether you should take a prescription medication or undergo nicotine replacement therapy in order to alleviate the withdrawal symptoms.

2. Learn to Recognize the Stress Warning Signs

Stress is frequently defined as a physical reaction to abrupt environmental alterations. Attempting to quit smoking is a significant transition that is disagreeable for almost everyone. Obviously, individuals respond to stress differently; what you find disagreeable may not be stressful for your sister or next-door neighbor.

Unfortunately, when you quit smoking, your stress level increases precisely at the time when you're giving up one of your coping mechanisms: smoking. When this occurs, you may experience the following symptoms of nicotine withdrawal:
Muscle tension

cervical and lumbar discomfort

Upset stomach

Headaches

Constipation or loose stools

Insufficiency of oxygen

Some individuals may experience insomnia, anxiety, depression, irritability, and fatigue. Learn to recognize your withdrawal symptoms, and make sure your friends and family are aware that you are experiencing them. If they understand your situation, they will be more willing to overlook your momentary discomfort.

Adopt Healthier Habits for Stress Relief

Some unpleasant situations are avoidable, while others are inevitable.

What matters most is how you approach them. Here are some techniques that may help you manage your stress.

Make contact with someone. A qualified counselor, empathetic acquaintance, support group, or family member may be able to offer you a fresh perspective on a challenging situation.

Deepen your respiration. Meditation, yoga, or other relaxation activities may help you manage a difficult situation. (Using a mindfulness application may also help combat tension.) Experiment with multiple methods, then settle on the most effective ones.

Get more exercise.

Working out reduces stress and may help improve your disposition. Try to incorporate a form of exercise that you enjoy into your daily routine.

Improve your diet. Consume regular meals and limit your coffee and alcohol intake.

Get outstanding shut-eye. Seven to nine hours of sleep per night is optimal.

Consider optimistic notions. Negativity and tension go hand in hand; therefore, make an effort to find the silver linings.
Do not overburden yourself with obligations. Establish boundaries with others and do not accept more work than you can handle. This is especially important during the first two months after quitting smoking.

Focus on what is essential. Focus on what must be done and learn to temporarily let go of other concerns.

The longer you refrain from smoking, the happier and certainly more tranquil you will become.

The Benefits Of Smoking

Cigarette smoking is believed to significantly reduce stress, help individuals unwind, concentrate, and increase mental capacity. Additionally, it acts as an antidepressant. It is one of the primary factors why people do not quit smoking. They fear that if they stopped, they would not be able to withstand the pressure from their careers or families. In anxious situations, smokers may choose cigarettes to alleviate their anxiety and help them make a decision. Even though smoking clogs their airways, their minds are sharper.

Smoking is an effective method for reducing hypertension. Cigarette smoke constricts the blood vessels in the pharynx and airways, resulting in a drop in blood pressure. Consequently, there are minimal to no risks of developing persistent hypertension. Cigarette smoking may reduce the risk of contracting this disease by approximately 30 percent.

Smoking cigarettes is also an effective way to reduce the risk of becoming obese. In the 1920s, cigarette companies promoted their product to women by promoting smoking as a "great way to lose weight." However, this does not suggest that one should smoke in order to lose weight. Nicotine is believed to aid in weight loss by decreasing appetite and desire.

Smoking breaks the atmosphere. Some individuals rely on smoking to socialize with others. Smoking may be perceived as a 'condition' for acceptance into a friend group. Therefore, it is easier for certain smokers to feel like they belong to a community. They need cigarettes to blend in.

Tobacco use significantly reduces or controls the incidence of Parkinson's disease. Compared to non-smokers, research indicates that the risk of Parkinson's disease is extremely low among smokers. This effect is attributable to the nicotine present in cigarettes. The incidence of Parkinson's disease is 41 percent lower among smokers.

The disadvantages of smoking

Lung cancer is the leading cause of death associated with smoking. It accounts for approximately 85 percent of all lung cancer cases. It harms not only smokers but also anyone exposed to secondhand smoke. Exposure to secondhand smoke may increase the risk of lung cancer in nonsmokers by 20 to 30 percent.

Tobacco use impairs the senses of smell and flavor. It alters the taste receptors, individuals lose their taste senses, and as a result, they lose their appetite and find bland foods appetizing.

Female smokers have increased difficulty conceiving. Additionally, they have an increased risk of miscarriage and premature labor. If the pregnancy is thankfully carried to term, the infant may be born with a cleft lip and cleft palate.

Smoking not only effects an individual's internal system, but also their external features. Cigarette smoke adheres to garments and hair. You can readily determine if a person has recently smoked or been around smokers. Additionally, teeth begin to yellow, and smoking may increase the likelihood of infections or inflammations that result in tooth and bone loss. Handling cigarettes stains the smoker's fingertips and fingernails.

Bronchitis is more probable among smokers. Nonsmokers exposed to secondhand smoke may also be affected, particularly children. Chronic coughs, also known as "smoker's cough," are a result of smoking's effect on the airways.

Developing a Mindset Free of Smoking

This book has thus far addressed the problem of smoking and its attendant complications. Now is the time to delve deeply into the core of the issue, your mind.

The psyche is an extremely potent entity. The psyche plays a role in so many aspects of our lives that we don't even have to be aware of it.

But when it comes to quitting smoking, you need to consider your mind (no pun intended) and realize how powerful it is in your battle to cease.

Reducing Your Desire for Cigarettes

When most people take their first inhalation, they immediately realize how disgusting it is. And yet, it appears that so many individuals are addicted from that point on.

Why do you even need to ask? It goes back to the concept of "following the crowd." When you light a cigarette and put it in your mouth, it doesn't matter how repulsive your body tells you it is; if your mind tells you it's acceptable, you will continue smoking.

The more cigarettes you smoke, even if your body doesn't like it, the more dependent you become on cigarettes, as your mind encourages you to continue smoking.

As one continues to smoke, he or she develops desires, which are difficult for the mind to resist.

The dictionary defines crave as "to long for or desire intensely" and "to require or need."

Your mind has convinced you that smoking is acceptable to the point that you smoke so frequently that your body becomes dependent on nicotine to function.

The more you smoke, the greater your demands for cigarettes become, until you can no longer live without so many cigarettes per day.

If you truly want to quit smoking, you will need to pay more attention to what your body is telling you about smoking than to what your mind is telling you.

How often have you been ill when you shouldn't have been, or laid up in bed when you should have been outside appreciating the beautiful weather? How many of these incidents do you believe were caused by your smoking habit?

Your body is a marvelous machine, but at some point it simply can't manage the toxins and foreign substances you're putting into it when you smoke, and it breaks down and ceases to function properly.

A crucial step on the road to quitting smoking is recognizing the nicotine craving you've developed and responding forcefully by starving it.

Refusing Your Body's Cravings Cravings? Sounds fairly severe, right? Well, if you think about it, it can't be much worse than lighting a cigarette on fire and inhaling nicotine and 4,000 other compounds while burning your lungs and affecting nearly every organ. In reality, this is precisely what you do every time you light a cigarette, despite the fact that it sounds incredibly graphic.

It is only when you consider smoking in this fashion that you can begin to change your mind.

It will be simpler for you to develop a mindset in which you have no desire to smoke if you have a clearer mental picture of how detrimental smoking is to your health.

Telling your body no is not a simple task. The word "no" consists of only two letters, yet saying it can be difficult, particularly when it comes to habits.

As you attempt to comprehend the harmful effects of smoking and the incredible freedom that comes with quitting, you will hopefully be able to develop the habit-breaking pattern of saying no to your cigarette inclinations.

Consider and Stop Smoking

Obviously, merely considering the issue will not solve your smoking problem. However, as has been explained, how you perceive it affects your attitude towards it.

Developing the correct mindset from the outset is the determining factor in ensuring your success on your endeavor to quit smoking. The dividing line between remaining a slave to your smoking addiction and experiencing the freedom of a life without tobacco rests within your own mind.

If you can develop a strong will to cease smoking as soon as possible, it will be much easier for you to do so.

Once you have begun to cultivate the correct mindset, it is time to investigate the various strategies for quitting nicotine.

Not every method will work for everyone, and you may find that one method works significantly better than the rest. The key is to discover what works and to persist with it.

Giving up cold turkey

By far, cold turkey is one of the most difficult methods for ceasing, yet it is the one that most people try first.

Although it is not unheard of for someone to decide one day to quit smoking and never handle tobacco again, this strategy does not always work for everyone. On average, approximately 90% of people who resolve to quit smoking attempt to do so by quitting abruptly.

However, less than 10% of these individuals typically prosper. This is not intended to discourage you, but rather to inform you that ceasing cold turkey may be one of the most difficult decisions you will make, as it will require a great deal of hard work, effort, and perseverance to achieve success.

On the other hand, there is something about quitting cold turkey that gives you a sense of accomplishment that you can be pleased with.

To be able to say that you made the decision one day to turn your back on cigarettes and never smoke again is a powerful motivator.

In addition, the experience you acquire can be extremely useful when trying to encourage a friend or family member who is also trying to quit nicotine.

There are a number of considerations to make before quitting cold turkey.

Take Each Step Separately

When transitioning from regular smoking to never smoking, quitting cold turkey is a significant change. Therefore, it is essential to take things one step and one day at a time.

Your body will rebel and tell you it needs a cigarette, and your mind may attempt to convince you that you can't continue, but you must persevere. You must go through each day knowing it will be difficult, but constantly reminding yourself that it is possible and worthwhile.

There may be times when the situation seems almost insufferable, but you must always be prepared for a deterioration.

However, if you take a long view, you will observe that it becomes progressively simpler over time. The journey is challenging, but you can make it!

Remove and Substitute Theory

Understanding the importance of not only removing something (such as cigarettes) from one's life, but also replacing it with something positive, is extremely beneficial when it comes to quitting cold turkey.

When you merely remove something, it requires more effort to adjust to its absence, whereas when you remove and replace with something positive, it satisfies that "need" in a sense.

When you cease smoking, you will find that you have more free time. The time you previously spent smoking will now need to be spent on something else.

When you find yourself with free time that you would have previously spent smoking, don't think about cigarettes; instead, fill that time with something else you truly appreciate.

Also, when it comes to removing, you must consider removing yourself, or avoiding places that would ordinarily encourage you to pull out a cigarette and light up.

If you cannot go outside during your break, locate a place where you can engage in an activity that will keep your mind as far away from smoking as possible.

Substituting positive experiences for negative ones is a crucial aspect of breaking any habit.

Rewarding Yourself

Rewarding yourself for success is a crucial component of overcoming your nicotine habit. Have you been smoke-free for one month?

Make it an occasion to celebrate! Have you made a deliberate decision to refrain from smoking? Then, treat yourself to a box of chocolates or anything else that strikes your fancy.

Rewarding yourself when you reach a significant milestone or make a decision that prevents you from smoking will be an important confidence booster as you progress.

Find peers or family members who will hold you accountable for achieving a specific objective, so they can celebrate with you and encourage you along the way.

Don't Quit

Don't give up on your journey to cease smoking! As you attempt to cease, you will undoubtedly encounter obstacles and challenges, but this should not deter you from doing what you know is best.

If quitting smoking cold turkey doesn't work, don't let that deter you from continuing to cease. Simply acknowledge that it does not work for you and then proceed to attempt something else.

As previously stated, there are numerous common solutions to smoking-related issues; you simply need to discover one that works for you.

Exercise:

Feel the sensation of water on your epidermis for a minimum of five minutes. This exercise can be performed in the shower, while washing your wands, taking a bath, swimming, walking in the rain, or by placing your hand in a basin filled with water. Close your eyes if you like.

How frequently do you intentionally encounter the essence of water? Every day, we take it for granted. It is a remarkable chemical substance that is essential for all life in the universe. Without it, none of us would exist. The capacity of this single transparent and fluid substance is enormous. The majority of your corporeal body is composed of this substance. Experience it.

On a daily basis, we take showers, wash our hands, and consume water, but we rarely take the time to appreciate our natural response to water. Water can provide the energy, sensation, actuality, and awareness of the present moment that cigarettes cannot. Water is an example of a positive dependency that does not bind you emotionally or spiritually, whereas smoking ties you to an unhealthy habit with dreadful long-term consequences.

Water can teach numerous teachings, including fluidity, flow, evaporation, change, motion, stillness, and life. You cannot learn any of these lessons through smoking or any other risky behavior.

*Ten minutes of silence and deliberate respiration. Repeat the mantra: "I am adaptable. I evolve. I circulate."

(Share your experience using the hashtag #30DaysWater)

Day 9

Exercise:

Close your mouth and eyes for five minutes while humming. Take long breaths between pauses. This exercise can be performed lying on a hard surface, standing, kneeling, or sitting with a straight back.

This exercise may appear trite, but there is much to learn from the sound of your voice during a prolonged murmur. Humming relaxes the body and mind, much like listening to raindrops, evening crickets, rustling foliage, or a waterfall. It is believed that the produced and continuously emitted wavelengths are responsible for this calming effect.

The most intriguing aspect of your humming, however, is that it is directly related to your respiration. If you take rapid, shallow breaths, your hum will be shorter and less effective; however, if you take deliberate, deep breaths, your hum will serve to calm your body and possibly bring you into the present moment. Additionally, did you observe that you were the one who was relaxing you? To become tranquil and still, you were not dependent on smoking cigarettes. You have the ability to soothe yourself without smoking.

Occasionally, listen to yourself murmur; observe the wavelengths that emanate from your own being. This is always accessible in the current instant.

*Ten minutes of silence and deliberate respiration. Repetition of the mantra: "Calmness and stillness are always present."

(Share this experience with the hashtag #30DaysHum)

Day 10

Exercise:

On a piece of paper (of any size), list the goals you've been striving to attain, i.e., the ones you believe will bring you happiness. For instance, a new job, a home in a pleasant neighborhood, traveling the world, a business, a family, new friends, a degree or certification, building a network, accumulating a million-dollar net worth, etc.

Now, rip the paper into several fragments and discard.

If not obsessively pursued, goals can be extremely useful and beneficial. In the modern world, however, individuals develop a dependence on goals. Consider all the times you've said, "I need to quit soon," "I must achieve this," "I'll do anything to achieve this," etc. Frequently, people spend more time worrying about their objectives than doing something spontaneously in the present to achieve them. In addition, the destination is ephemeral, whereas the journey in the present moment is genuine and enduring.

Dependencies imperceptibly inculcate the mentality that objectives must be achieved or else failure will result. When you endeavored to stop smoking in the past, what was your objective? What did you feel you needed to accomplish? Did you attribute your value to the achievement of this objective? You do not need to attain a goal in order to quit smoking; you can quit immediately.

*Ten minutes of silence and deliberate respiration. Repetition of the mantra: "Achieving an objective does not affect my happiness. Now I'm satisfied."

(Share this experience with the hashtag #30DaysGoals)

Day 11

Exercise:

Compress the skin on the back of your hand or forearm until you feel minor discomfort and pain. It is not necessary to pinch yourself firmly enough to bleed; a small burn is sufficient.

Did I cause your discomfort by requesting that you perform this exercise? No; you brought this suffering upon yourself; consider this thoughtfully. You even chose how much agony to inflict upon yourself and when to relieve it. You cannot accuse me or anyone else for your current suffering. You alone were culpable. You were responsible for letting go, as well.

This is readily comprehended in terms of physical pain, such as pinching oneself; however, we have great difficulty comprehending this lesson in terms of negative emotions and feelings. How frequently have you and others said, "He makes me so angry when...", "I'm depressed because she...", or "I'm so frustrated that they..."? Nobody ever forces you to experience negative emotions. You are always the one experiencing problems and then assigning responsibility to others. You are essentially emotionally squeezing yourself and refusing to let go.

People use cigarettes to alleviate pain for their complete lives. Instead of letting go, they scream, "Release the pain!" at others. Let go! Mend this! Stop doing this! You are responsible!" Wake up and realize that you alone are responsible for letting go of the anguish, and that you can do so without using cigarettes.

*Ten minutes of silence and deliberate respiration. Repeat the mantra: "I can let go of negative emotions right now."

(Share this experience with the hashtag #30DaysPinch)

Day 12

Exercise:

Spend five minutes inhaling an aromatic object, such as a piece of fruit, a spice, tea, pine, cedar, a flower, or a scented candle. Five minutes must be spent concentrating on the scent of that one item. Nothing should deflect you from the scent.

How often do you take the time to appreciate a pleasant scent? One of the myths of modern society is that if you indulge your senses for too long, you will lose out on _____. While people are rushing toward their objectives with elevated stress levels, they are completely unaware of the present moment. People look at images of food that others have posted on the internet, but they do not take the time to scent and taste actual food in the present.

Which is preferable: inhaling toxic cigarette smoke and smelling like a chimney, or appreciating the aroma of vanilla, citrus, or pine in the present? The first is fictitious and deceptive, while the second is authentic and sensational. Smoking effectively depletes time and energy from other senses, such as scent. Focusing on smell and utilizing your other senses is one of the most effective methods to return to the present moment and abandon illusions. No longer permit smoking to diminish your other senses. Awaken your sense of scent.

Why Stop Smoking? How? And Right This Minute!

Quitting smoking is challenging. The following advice may assist you in quitting smoking.

Create a list of your reasons for quitting and carry it with you. Review the list whenever you feel the urge to smoke.

Set a date for quitting and quit completely. Some individuals favor the notion of cutting back gradually. However, research indicates that if you consume fewer cigarettes than usual, you are more likely to smoke more of each cigarette, resulting in nicotine levels that are nearly identical.

Consequently, it is best to cease entirely on a specified date.

Inform everyone that you have decided to cease smoking. Friends and family typically provide support and assistance. If other members of your household smoke, quitting will be more difficult; therefore, if possible, attempt to convince other household members or friends who smoke to quit at the same time. Individual effort may be more difficult than teamwork.

Remove all cigarettes, ashtrays, and lighters from your residence.

Expect withdrawal symptoms. When you quit smoking, you may experience symptoms such as nausea (feeling ill), migraines, anxiety, irritation, cravings, and an overall awful disposition. These symptoms are caused by the absence of nicotine, to which your body has become accustomed. They typically reach their peak within 12 to 24 hours, then decline progressively over the course of two to four weeks.

Get ready to wheeze. It is common for a smoker's cough to significantly worsen after quitting smoking (as the airways "returned to life"). Numerous individuals claim that this makes them feel worse for a time after quitting smoking and makes them contemplate resuming the habit. Resist this enticement! Usually, the wheezing improves over time.

Consider the circumstances in which you are likely to want to smoke. In particular, alcohol consumption is commonly associated with failure to quit smoking. During the first few weeks after quitting smoking, you must avoid consuming excessive amounts of alcohol. Alter your daily regimen for the first few weeks. For example, if "the social club" is an alluring place to smoke and consume alcohol, avoid it for a while. Similarly, if drinking tea and coffee is also associated with smoking, consider substituting them with fruit juice and lots of water.

Take one day at a time and mark each day of accomplishment on a calendar. Check it out when you feel the urge to smoke, and convince yourself that you DO NOT want to start smoking again.

Declare the subsequent:

You can tell others that you do not smoke.

You will smell much healthier

After a few weeks, you will feel much better, have a much improved sense of taste, and cough less. You will also have more money.

You can purchase indulgences with the money you would have spent on cigarettes.

Some people worry about acquiring weight when they quit smoking because their appetite may increase. Expect an increase in appetites, but avoid snacking on fatty or sugary foods. Try gum without sugar and fruit instead.

Don't despair if you fall short. Examine why you felt it was more difficult at a particular time; this will make you stronger for the future. Typically, those who successfully quit smoking have made three or four prior attempts.

How to Give Up Smoking Efficiently

1) Quitting smoking is not as difficult as you may believe.

When you begin to be sincere and examine the facts about smoking, it will become a delight to rid yourself of this addiction.

Consider your smoking habit objectively; evaluate it with sincerity. Ask precisely what it is providing, and then consider what it is not providing. Additionally, you could start with your hair and work your way down to your toenails. It is a medical fact that smoking has negative effects on every organ in the human body.

2) Consider quitting cigarettes as a GIANT gift to yourself.

You are substantially improving your quality of life and almost certainly extending your lifespan. You are making your body healthier. You are gaining conviction in yourself. You are gifting yourself all the money you previously spent on not only the cost of cigarettes, but also the additional premium increases and loaded points for health insurance and life insurance. Wrap it all up, recognize it as the gift that it is, and go for it!

3) Set a date

Make a commitment. Test it out. Remember that it's okay if you don't succeed at first, but be sure to keep attempting. You can only lose if you give up attempting. If you are not yet prepared to set a date for quitting, work on yourself to develop the desire.

4) Do not consider yourself to be "giving up" something.

This makes the loss appear excessive. What you are actually doing is discarding something from your life that has caused you harm and has no place in your life anymore. You are throwing away unadulterated garbage. No longer will nicotine and tars be permitted to reside in your alveoli.

5) Always maintain a good mindset

This is among the most beneficial actions you've ever taken. Avoid negative or hostile individuals and uncomfortable situations.

6) Quit independently.

Even though your family and loved ones will benefit tremendously from your quitting, you will benefit the most. Consider quitting smoking with the respect it justly merits. Be willing to take any measures necessary to eliminate it from your life.

What exactly is nicotine?

Look up the term 'nicotine' in the dictionary and record its definition in LARGE letters. "A poisonous alkaloid utilized as a pesticide.' Put it where it can be seen.

8) Do not deceive yourself by claiming you have too many stresses in your life to quit smoking.

If you are a smoker, you are under a tremendous amount of pressure. As a result of smoking, daily life is a gamble, as is your future existence. By eliminating nicotine from your life, you will find it simpler to manage a variety of other issues. You will feel significantly better and have more vitality. You will have established something significantly more meaningful than wealth and opulence ever could. You will have provided something that no one else can provide. You will not be subject to the pressures of smoking.

9) Do not use the possibility of gaining weight to justify smoking.

If you do gain a little bit of weight, the fact that you will be more active, have more vitality, and exercise will offset any concerns regarding weight gain. Remember that gluttony, not smoking, is the cause of weight gain.

10) Plan activities that will distract you from consuming

Sometimes, the psyche can be our greatest enemy. They will claim that we need a cigarette for practically any reason that is expedient at the time. Consider engaging in activities that will distract you from smoking, such as going to the movies, visiting museums, swimming, working out at the gym, or accessing public buildings that are generally smoke-free. These activities will help keep you occupied, free of temptations, and strengthen your resolve to quit smoking.

11) Do not expose yourself to smoke-filled environments.

If you discover yourself in the company of a smoker, simply ask to be excused. "He/She is smoking the cigarette I might be smoking," then be thankful you do not have to smoke it.

Expecting a smoke-free public space has become much more socially acceptable, while smoking in public has become much more socially unacceptable.

12) While you are pausing, think of it as an investment.

Once you have abstained for one hour, you have spent this time becoming a healthier individual. Now, invest an additional hour. Hourly progress on your investment. It will become less difficult and feel better as the hours pass. You will begin to observe and experience the increasing benefits of this investment. Protect your investment as you would a priceless relic.

Be kind to yourself; it is the start of a new lifestyle. Remember that you are not continuously introducing contaminants into your system, and treat yourself with respect and enthusiasm. Deeply inhale only clean oxygen. Examine the various fragrances. Spend time in nature. You will have numerous new experiences.

13) Do not get upset, hungry, exhausted or lonely

If we are anxious, stressed, or furious, our minds tell us that smoking will help us cope. Until your mind realizes that it can function without cigarettes, you should avoid situations that could cause you distress. Avoid certain individuals who annoy you. If there is a great deal of tension at work, you should attempt to take a few days off. If you cannot take a significant amount of time off, cease smoking over a long weekend. Avoid as much as possible situations such as getting trapped in heavy traffic. Use exceptional caution. Anger can be extremely damaging.

Do not be famished or hungry. It is remarkable how our minds can convince us that everything is wrong and that smoking will help, when all we need to do is eat.

Don't be too exhausted. If we are exhausted, it is easy to become irritable, and when we become agitated, our minds will tell us that smoking will help. Our resistance may be weakened, making it simple to conclude, "Oh well, I guess I'll smoke."

You should not feel alone as you cease smoking. It is beneficial to comprehend others who are experiencing the same situation. By attending Nicotine Anonymous conferences, you can encounter individuals in a similar situation.

You could remember the aforementioned four concerns by the acronym "HALT." Hungry - angry - lonely - exhausted. If you discover yourself approaching any of the above, yell "STOP."

14) Prevent yourself from becoming weary.

It can be difficult to merely sit without smoking. Keep occupied. Find activities that you find enjoyable. Cycling, hiking, swimming, jogging, traveling, and attempting new restaurants are merely a few examples. Now is the moment for self-indulgence!

Have something to twiddle. If we are acclimated to holding a cigarette, our hands may crave something when we are unable to do so. Hold a small rubber ball, yo-yo, pen, or perhaps Play Dough.

Have something available for consumption. Life Savers are good or any sort of gradually liquefying candy. Additionally, beef jerky and lollipops may aid. Avoid fattening foods like pastries. While you are still smoking, experiment to determine what will alleviate the craving. If Life Savers are effective, stockpile them. A word of caution: these 'substitutes' should only be used temporarily.

15) Eliminate beverages linked to smoking

Do not consume alcohol while ceasing. As soon as alcohol enters the system, a person's defenses significantly weaken. Similarly, if you are accustomed to consuming tea, coffee, or other beverages while smoking, you should eliminate these beverages prior to quitting.

Remember that the discomfort you experience during the first two weeks is only temporary. You will never have to experience it again!

16) Congratulate yourself frequently.

Quitting smoking is not an easy task; it requires a great deal of courage to attempt to do so. If you are experiencing withdrawal discomfort, let it serve as a lasting reminder of how potent nicotine is and how dependent you were on it. Consider that every minute you sucked on cigarettes, they were sucking on you. They were literally squeezing your vitality out of you. Don't allow this to occur any longer.

17) Avoid the temptation of self-pity

If we begin to feel miserable for ourselves, our minds will convince us that smoking will help us feel better. Remember that if you persist in your efforts to cease, you will succeed. Favorable probabilities are in your favor.

Plan your activities for the first few days after quitting before quitting. Thus, you will not be required to make many decisions during the withdrawal process.

Remember that the first cigarette is what starts you smoking. It takes just one. This is the one that you do not want. You can always delay igniting the first cigarette for a while. Do not fool yourself into believing that you can halt and start at will. You cannot. Many individuals have attempted this but have been unable to quit nicotine completely.

If you do not intend to cease immediately and completely, reduce your consumption. If you smoke two packs per day and reduce your consumption by one cigarette per day for a month, you will smoke ten cigarettes per day. However, the recommendation is to designate a date and quit completely, as opposed to quitting gradually.

18) Drink loads of fluids

Fluids help remove toxins from your system. Given that smoking diminishes vitamin C levels in the body, orange juice is superb.

19) Remind yourself frequently of the following Happy News

Your breath does not have a stale ashtray odor.

Your teeth are beginning to shed their yellow hue and appear white and intense.

You have not stained your fingertips with tobacco.

The wheezing of that cigarette smoker who appeared ill is diminishing.

Your scent and taste senses are returning.

Your complexion is beginning to improve.

Your general self-perception is significantly improved.

You are starting to care deeply about yourself.

20. Provide direction to others

Please offer support, guidance, and encouragement to others who may be struggling to quit smoking whenever you have the chance. Supporting others in this endeavor will strengthen your resolve to abstain from nicotine. There is great reward in assisting another individual in gaining freedom from this detrimental substance.

21) Implement a follow-up plan

Do not assume that if you have endured a few weeks without smoking, you have completely overcome the temptation to smoke. Nicotine is extremely cunning. If possible, continue attending Nicotine Anonymous meetings. If there are no meetings in your area, you might consider starting one. It is very simple. You only need a room and a few interested individuals.

Giving up results in vastly superior sex:

Quitting smoking improves the body's blood circulation, thereby increasing sensitivity. Men who stop smoking may experience improved erections. Women may find that their climaxes improve and they are significantly more readily attracted. It has also been found that nonsmokers are three times more alluring to potential partners than tobacco smokers (possibly one of the benefits of smelling clean).

Cessation of smoking increases fertility:

Non-smokers conceive much more easily than smokers. Quitting smoking improves the lining of the uterus and can increase the potency of men's sperm. Being a nonsmoker increases the likelihood of conceiving through IVF and decreases the likelihood of a miscarriage. Most importantly, it increases the likelihood of having a healthy infant.

Nonsmokers have epidermis that appears more youthful:

Smoking cessation has been shown to reduce facial aging and delay the appearance of wrinkles. A nonsmoker's skin receives more nutrients, including oxygen, and can rectify the sallow, wrinkled skin that smokers typically have.

Nonsmokers' teeth are whiter and their breath is fresher:

Stopping smoking prevents tooth discoloration. Ex-smokers are less likely than current smokers to suffer from periodontal disease and premature tooth loss.

Quitting smoking enables for easier breathing:

Ex-smokers breathe more readily and cough less after quitting smoking because their lung capacity increases by as much as 10 percent within nine months. In your twenties and thirties, the effect of smoking on your lung capacity may not be noticeable until you begin running, but lung capacity decreases naturally with age. Having maximum lung capacity in later years can be the difference between an active, healthy seniorhood and hissing when walking or ascending stairs.

Stop smoking to extend your life:

Half of all long-term cigarette smokers perish prematurely from smoking-related illnesses, such as coronary artery disease, lung cancer, and chronic bronchitis. Men who cease smoking by age 30 gain ten years of life. Those who quit smoking at age 60 gain three years of life. It is never too late to benefit from ceasing smoking. Not only does quitting add years to your life, but it also substantially increases the likelihood of a mobile, healthy, and happy seniorhood.

Stop smoking and you'll experience less stress:

After quitting smoking, anxiety levels are lower, according to scientific studies. Pure nicotine addiction causes smokers to experience 'drawback' symptoms between cigarettes. The transient pleasure derived from satisfying a craving is not an effective remedy for stress. In addition, as a result of the increased oxygen levels in the body, ex-smokers are able to concentrate better, have better mental health, and enjoy greater overall health.

Quitting smoking enhances vitality, immunity, and the senses of scent and taste:

Quitting smoking improves your senses of smell and flavor. The body is recovering from the debilitating effects of the hundreds of toxic compounds found in cigarettes. Quitting smoking also increases your vitality levels. Within two to twelve weeks of quitting smoking, your blood circulation improves, making all forms of exercise, including walking and running, considerably simpler.

Quitting smoking strengthens the immune system, making it simpler to combat colds and influenza. The increase in oxygen in the body makes former smokers less fatigued and less susceptible to migraines.

Smoke-free dwellings safeguard your family:

By quitting smoking, you will protect the health of your loved ones who do not smoke. Passive smoking increases the risk of lung cancer, heart disease, and stroke in nonsmokers. Secondhand smoke increases the risk of respiratory diseases in children, including pneumonia, croup (inflamed airways in the lungs), and bronchitis, as well as ear infections, coughing, and asthma. Children who live with smokers are three times more likely to develop lung cancer in adulthood than children who live with nonsmokers.

What Is The "Right" Way To Stop Smoking?

Before we delve into the step-by-step process of the book, let's take a moment to discuss the most common smoking cessation methods. Since each has advantages and disadvantages, we have incorporated multiple approaches into our habit framework.

Let's examine five of the most prevalent methods for quitting smoking:

#1: Going "cold turkey" and relying solely on fortitude.

You quit smoking immediately. You discard any remaining cigarettes and make the decision to quit smoking immediately. The instant of resignation is unambiguous.

Pros: you can start immediately, there is no slow weaning-off period, there is a distinct quit date, it is free, and you can start it today.

Cons: grapple with physical and mental dependency

One slip-up with a cigarette can cause this method to become extremely fragile. When you make a mistake with this method, you tend to blame yourself, which can make it more difficult to attempt again.

Using nicotine aids such as gum, the patch, or similar products.

This is a delayed method that gives you time to manage your cravings. First, you supplant cigarettes with a nicotine-containing alternative, and then, over time, you gradually reduce your nicotine intake.

Helps you deal with both chemical and psychological addiction separately; gradually weans you off nicotine addiction; separates physical addiction from the act of smoking; scientifically designed to be highly effective

Cons: can be quite costly and leaves you addicted to the high of nicotine even after quitting smoking.

#3: Utilizing a robust support network.

Join a support group or surround yourself with other people who have ceased smoking to help you stay on track. Similar to the effects of Alcoholics Anonymous membership.

People are always there to support you, so you never feel alone. Quitting is regarded as a process, which relieves stress and reduces the risk of self-blame.

Cons: your support network isn't always there with you; if someone in your support network messes up, they can bring you down with them; you become reliant on an external source of confidence; you can quit without building the proper psychological infrastructure, leading to relapse; and you can quit without building the correct psychological infrastructure, leading to relapse.

Taking a prescription medication ranks fourth.

There are very potent medications containing the active constituent varenicline, such as Chantix. It functions by stimulating the portion of the brain that relishes nicotine and preventing nicotine from attaching to the receptors in that region.

Cons: requires a doctor's assistance and a customized plan based on your current smoking addiction, but it is the most effective method to get you (as an individual) free of nicotine addiction.

Negatives: costly, replaces one chemical dependency with another, and may have side effects that contribute to additional health issues.

5. Using an electronic cigarette.

Electronic cigarettes heat a liquid, which may or may not contain nicotine, to produce vapor as opposed to smoke (imagine steam from simmering water).

Pros: you can vape in many places where smoking is prohibited; it allows you to maintain the physical habit without the addiction habit; it's a very fast and effective technique that allows you to gradually wean yourself off the most dangerous chemicals in cigarettes; and it's a relatively inexpensive alternative to smoking.

Negative: can be astronomically expensive

You're giving your money to the exact same company that was poisoning you in the first place. You replace one version of smoking with another; you still have this habit that is, at best, neutral. You're reliant on technology, and if technology fails, you will fail. If your vaping battery expires and you must purchase an expensive replacement, you may revert to smoking cigarettes.

Now, before we continue, I'd like to devote a separate section to the potential dangers of vaping; vaping is such a novel habit that no one is certain of its long-term effects. Vaping may turn out to be as terrible as or even worse than smoking, so I list it here as a temporary alternative to smoking, but I do not recommend it for long-term use.

The FDA has taken significant measures to protect Americans from the dangers of tobacco by implementing new regulations, which also apply to e-cigarettes. Vaping is classified as addictive and is prohibited for those under the age of 18.

The following adverse effects have been associated with vaping:

dryness of the pharynx

sore gums

- Dizziness
- Cough
- Dry epidermis
- Itchiness
- Dry eyes
- Nosebleeds
- Bleeding gums
- Headache
- Throbbing inflammation of the tongue
- Black mouth
- Sleepiness
- Sleeplessness
- Allergies
- Chest discomfort
- breathing difficulties

Even though it is referred to as "vaping," only a small portion of what is inhaled is water vapor. Previous research has demonstrated that propylene glycol can cause eye and respiratory irritation. The Dow Chemical Company recommends individuals avoid inhaling propylene glycol in its assessment of the product's safety.

New research published in Nicotine & Tobacco Research by Goniewicz and associates reveals that potentially toxic carbonyls can form when e-liquids are heated at high temperatures, with levels of carcinogenic formaldehyde comparable to those found in tobacco smoke. Lastly, some of the flavorings in electronic cigarettes can be toxic.

How to Create the Ideal Plan for Yourself

The majority of quit-smoking plans, strategies, tactics, and methods focus on eliminating the nicotine habit. Vaping is the most popular method (and currently, the majority of people find it to be the best and most effective method) because it employs replacement ideology, replacing a negative habit with a good one.

If none of the aforementioned techniques seem to fit your needs, don't be afraid to attempt something more unconventional. Join a Facebook group (such as ours) and ask other members what methods they're attempting. Conduct some research, consult with individuals who have successfully ceased smoking, and conduct some additional research. Some individuals were able to quit using unconventional methods, such as hypnosis, self-talk, Pilates, or even laser therapy, but the only thing that matters is that they were successful.

According to one of our viewers, he had tried everything but nothing had worked. Even though he was not a member, he joined a Seventh-day Adventist Church program out of desperation. After five days of seminars in which they demonstrated some very specific techniques (such as the cold mitten friction technique, having a buddy, and changing where you typically sit, among other ideas), he quit smoking and has not touched a cigarette since.

As we move forward, our focus will be on incorporating the techniques that work best for you into an overall plan to develop a healthy lifestyle, one small habit at a time.

Considering the advantages and disadvantages of the aforementioned common alternatives, you may be willing to employ some but not others. Our objective is to get you to a point where none of these habits—chewing gum, vaping, or patches—stand between you and your addiction. Instead, we will completely supplant this practice. You will be on the path to prosperity, and you will lose your desire to smoke. We'll eliminate the temptation at its source so that you don't have to struggle through this process; instead, you'll find that it's both emotionally and practically effortless.

Examine this list to determine which of these methods you are familiar with and which you are not. CDC research indicates that combining methodologies is the most effective strategy. When deeply mired in the path of addiction, a combination of resolve, emotional support, and the involvement of a medical professional can be the triumvirate of success.

There is no single optimal solution that is effective for everyone. Instead, we will provide you with a framework that you can adapt to your specific circumstances.

www.ingramcontent.com/pod-product-compliance
Lightning Source LLC
Chambersburg PA
CBHW050236120526
44590CB00016B/2113